Book of Saints
"SUPERHEROES OF GOD"

By REV. LAWRENCE G. LOVASIK, S.V.D.
Divine Word Missionary

PART 5

D0559060

CONTENTS

NIHIL OBSTAT: Daniel V. Flynn, J.C.D., *Censor Librorum*
IMPRIMATUR: ✝ Joseph T. O'Keefe, D.D.,
Vicar General, Archdiocese of New York

Printed in China   ISBN 978-0-89942-393-7
CPSIA   March 2019   10 9 8 7 6 5 4 3 2   L/P

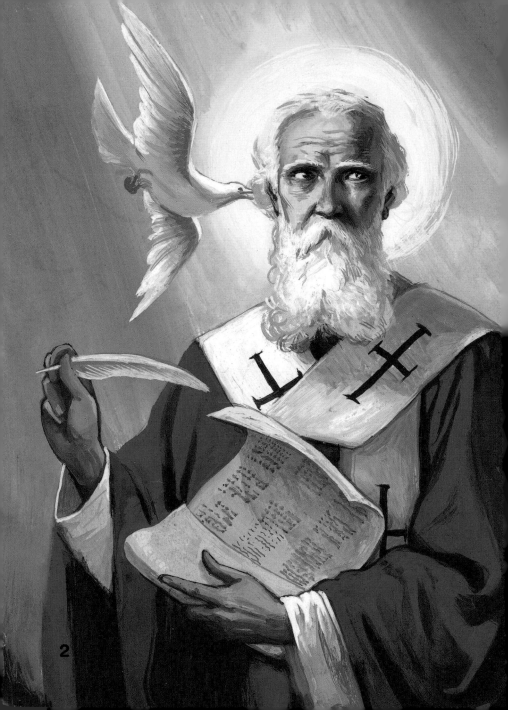

Saint Basil the Great

January 2

B ASIL was born at Caesarea, in Asia Minor, in the year 329. His mother and father were nobles and also Saints. There were ten children in the family, four of whom became Saints.

Basil went to school in Constantinople and then in Athens, and later became an eloquent lawyer in Caesarea. But he felt that God called him to become a monk. He sold all his goods, gave the money to the poor, and became a monk.

Basil visited the monks who lived in the desert and founded several monasteries. He drew up rules for the monks to lead them to holiness. Although he was in poor health, Basil lived a life of penance and prayer.

Basil became the Archbishop of Caesarea and defended this people against the Roman Emperor.

Basil wrote many books and defended the Church against the Arian heretics. He was given the titles "Doctor of the Church," and "Father of the Church." Basil died in the year 379.

Saint Anthony the Abbot

A NTHONY was born in Egypt in the year 251. While still a young man, he gave away all his goods and begged an old hermit to teach him how to live a holy life. He lived the life of a hermit in the desert for many years, devoting himself to prayer and penance.

Many people came to Anthony for advice. He taught them the way to holiness. He founded a monastery and was the first Abbot to form a rule for his family of monks dedicated to Divine Service. For this reason he is called the "Patriarch of Monks."

His miracles drew so many people to him that he fled again into the desert where he lived by hard work and prayer.

In the year 305, Anthony founded a religious community of hermits who lived in separate cells.

He died in 356, at 105 years of age.

Anthony is called the Father of monastic life.

Saint Isidore of Seville

April 4

ISIDORE was born at Cartagena in Spain. His two brothers and sisters are Saints. As a boy Isidore was discouraged because he failed in his studies, but with the help of God he became one of the most learned men of his time.

Isidore helped to free Spain from the Arian heresy. Following a call from God, he became a hermit. But after his brother's death he became the Archbishop of Seville. Both of his brothers were bishops.

Isidore was admired for his preaching, his miracles, his work for the liturgy and the laws of the Church. He brought many Catholics in Spain back to the Church. He was the head of the Fourth Council of the Church in Toledo in 633.

Isidore wrote many books. He governed his diocese about thirty-seven years. He died in Seville on April 4, 636. He is honored as a Doctor of the Church.

Saint Vincent Ferrer

April 5

VINCENT was born in Valencia, Spain, January 23, 1350. He was educated at the Dominican school in Barcelona and later entered the Order. He became a doctor of sacred theology.

Vincent devoted himself to missionary work and preached in nearly every province of Spain. He also preached in France, Italy, Germany, Holland, England, Scotland, and Ireland. Many conversions followed his preaching. He is one of the most famous missionaries of the fourteenth century.

Vincent's main virtues were humility and the spirit of prayer, which made his work successful. His motto was: "Whatever you do, think not of yourself, but of God."

His wonderful missionary work lasted twenty-one years. He died in France on April 5, 1419.

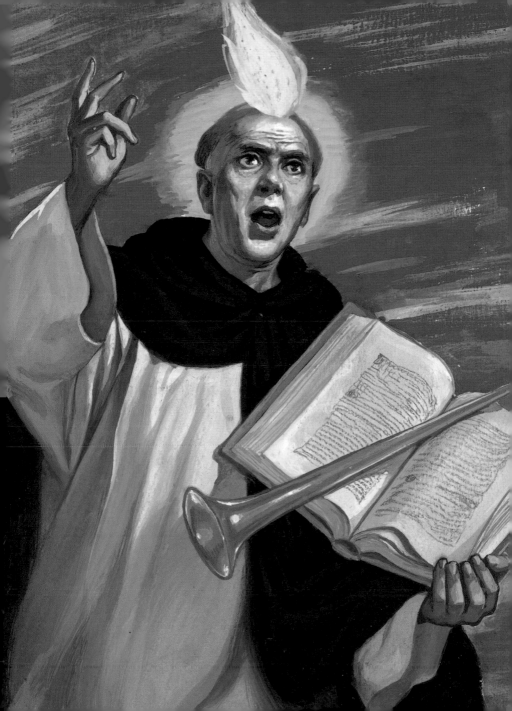

Saint Gemma Galgani

April 11

G EMMA was born near Lucca, Italy, in 1878. At the age of twenty she had an incurable tuberculosis of the spine. Through her prayers to St. Gabriel of the Sorrowful Mother, she was cured.

Gemma tried to became a Passionist nun, but was rejected. She was again stricken with an illness. She lived a very prayerful life and suffered patiently. She said: "Jesus, I can bear no more. If it be Your holy will, take me."

Gemma died on April 11, 1903, as she lifted her eyes to a picture of the Blessed Virgin Mary and said: "Mother, I give my soul into your hands. Ask Jesus to be merciful to me." She was only twenty-five years of age.

Gemma's remains are in the chapel of the Passionist Sisters in Lucca. A table at her tomb states that she was more consumed by the fire of divine love than by her wasting disease.

Saint Philip Neri

May 26

PHILIP was born in Florence in 1515. His family was poor. He went to Rome to act as a teacher for two boys. He began to visit the hospitals of the city, taking a great interest in the sick and the poor.

Philip was ordained a priest and founded the Congregation of the Priests of the Oratory. With his priests he helped the boys of Rome when they were in trouble. He found places for them to study and to play. He showed great zeal in helping sinners through the Sacrament of Penance.

Philip encouraged frequent Confession and Communion. Young and old, attracted by his cheerful holiness, came in large numbers to hear his words of wisdom.

For sixty-two years Philip gave advice and a good example to all classes of people in Rome and tried to fill their hearts with the love of God.

Philip died at the age of 80 in 1595.

Saint Camillus de Lellis

CAMILLUS was born in Italy in 1550. As a young man he became a soldier and led a wayward life. He lost so much in gambling that he was forced to work on a building which belonged to the Capuchins.

He was converted and tried three times to enter the Capuchin Order, but each time a wound in his leg forced him to leave. He went to Rome for medical treatment, and there took St. Philip Neri as his confessor.

Camillus entered the hospital for incurables. Later he had charge of it. At the age of thirty-two, he began to study grammar with children.

Of the noble family of Lellis, Camillus, when still a young priest, consecrated his life to the service of the sick. He founded the Order of Hospitallers, or the Congregation of the Servants of the Sick. The Brothers served the sick not only in hospitals but also in their homes.

Camillus died a victim of his charity in 1614.

Saint Christopher

July 25

THERE is a legend that in the land of Canaan in Palestine there lived a very strong man called Offero. He is said to have left his native land looking for adventure. He said: "I will roam through the whole world in search of the greatest of kings, and I will be his servant."

Offero met a hermit who guarded a dangerous passage across a stream, and guided travelers to a place where they could cross safely. The hermit instructed him about our Lord, the greatest King. Offero settled down near the stream and carried travelers across on his shoulders to serve the great King.

One day he carried a little boy on his shoulders. Offero cried out: "Child, I feel as if I were carrying the whole world upon my shoulders."

The little boy answered smiling: "You are carrying more than the world; you are carrying Him Who created heaven and earth." It is said that the boy Jesus baptized Offero. Since then he is called Christopher or Christ-bearer.

Saint Ignatius of Loyola

July 31

IGNATIUS, born in 1491 at the royal Castle of Loyola, Spain, became a knight in the court of King Ferdinand V. Wounded in the siege of Pampeluna, he lay ill in a castle, where he picked up a book of the Lives of the Saints and started to read.

When he left the castle, he went to confession. For almost a year he lived in a cave on the banks of a river. He fasted, prayed, and took care of the poor and the sick.

A man of thirty-five years of age, he entered a school in Barcelona, Spain. After being ordained a priest, he founded the Society of Jesus at Paris. Schools, preaching, retreats, missionary work— any work was to be their work, especially at a time when many were falling away from the Church. Many of his men became missionaries, and some taught the Indians in America.

For fifteen years Ignatius directed the work of the Society. Almost blind, he died at the age of sixty-five on July 31, 1556.

Saint John Eudes

August 19

JOHN Eudes was born in France, November 14, 1601. As a priest he was full of zeal for the salvation of souls. During a plague he spent two months ministering to the sick and dying.

John preached as a missionary among the people in France for ten years.

His great work was in starting seminaries for the education of priests. He founded the Congregation of Priests of Jesus and Mary to form virtuous priests in seminaries. They wore a badge on which were inscribed the hearts of Jesus and Mary. They were also called Eudists.

John also founded the Congregation of the Sisters of Our Lady of Charity to work for penitent women.

John spread devotion to the Sacred Hearts of Jesus and Mary. He died in 1680.

Saint Gregory the Great

G REGORY was born in the year 540. He was the son of a wealthy Roman senator, who sent him to the best teachers. His mother was St. Silvia.

Gregory sold his property and built six monasteries in Sicily and one in Rome, where he went to live as a monk. But he continued his kind deeds to help the needy.

Gregory was sent as a missionary to England by the Pope. Later he was elected Pope and sent St. Augustine and a company of monks to England in 597. He also sent missionaries to France, Spain, and Africa.

Gregory is called "Great" above all because of the many books he wrote on the liturgy. He is also honored as Doctor of the Church because of his great learning. He made wise laws to govern the Church.

Gregory was a Benedictine. He died in the year 604.

Saint Robert Bellarmine

September 17

ROBERT was born in Italy in 1542. He joined the Society of Jesus. Although ill health was his cross all during his life, he became the great defender of the Church against the followers of the Protestant Reformation.

Robert wrote many books that were read by Catholics and Protestants. He wrote two famous catechisms, which were much used in the Church.

Having become a cardinal, he laid aside his books and began preaching to the people, teaching catechism to the children, visiting the sick, and helping the poor.

But three years later Pope Paul V always had Cardinal Bellarmine at his side. As a member of almost every Congregation at the Vatican, he played an important part in the affairs of the Holy See.

He died at the age of seventy-nine in 1621. He is honored as a Doctor of the Church because of his great learning.

Saint Paul of the Cross

P AUL was born in Genoa, Italy, on January 3, 1694. After his ordination he was inspired in a vision to found a congregation in honor of the Passion of Jesus Christ. He was invested by the bishop with the habit that had been shown to him in the vision.

Paul chose as the badge of his congregation a heart with three nails, in memory of the sufferings of Jesus. The Rule he wrote was approved by Benedict XIV. A large community of the Passionists lived at the Church of Saints John and Paul in Rome.

The work of the Passionists was preaching to the people in parishes. For fifty years Paul remained the untiring missionary of Italy. He believed himself to be a useless servant and a great sinner, though God granted him many wonderful gifts of soul.

Paul died at Rome in the year 1775, at the age of eighty-one.

Saint Leo the Great

November 10

L EO was born in Tuscany in Italy. He reigned as Pope from 440 to 461. At this time Attila, called the Scourge of God, with his hordes of Huns invaded Italy and marched toward Rome.

Moved with pity for his suffering people, Leo went out to meet him. His pleading persuaded the invader to leave Rome.

Later, when Genseric, another invader, entered Rome, Leo's holiness and eloquence again saved the city.

Heresies attacked the Church. Leo called the Council of Chalcedon and condemned them.

The holy Pope built many churches. He left many letters and writings of great historical value. For this reason, but especially for his holiness, he is called "the Great." He is honored as a Doctor of the Church.

Leo died on April 11, 461.

Saint Peter Canisius

PETER was born in Holland on May 8, 1521. He became a Jesuit. St. Ignatius kept him by his side for five months. On the day of his final vows, as he knelt in St. Peter's Basilica in Rome, he was favored with a vision of the Sacred Heart. From that time he never failed to make an offering of all his work to the Sacred Heart of Jesus.

Peter became known for his preaching and writing. He was sent to Germany where he attacked heretical teaching. He wrote a catechism which was translated into many languages. He founded a number of colleges.

Peter was the second great Apostle of Germany, the first being St. Boniface. He was one of the greatest opponents of the Reformation through his preaching and writing of books in defense of the Faith.

Peter died in Switzerland in 1597. Pope Pius XI canonized him in 1925 and proclaimed him a Doctor of the Church.

A Prayer of the Church

B Y your gift we celebrate the festival of your city,
the heavenly Jerusalem, our mother,
where the great array of our brothers and sisters
already gives you eternal praise.

Towards her, we eagerly hasten
as pilgrims advancing by faith,
rejoicing in the glory bestowed upon
those exalted members of the Church
through whom you give us, in our frailty,
both strength and good example.

(From the Preface for the Solemnity
of All Saints, November 1)